Departure

A Play

Stephen Smith

Samuel French – London
New York – Sydney – Toronto – Hollywood

Copyright © 1989 by STEPHEN SMITH
All Rights Reserved

DEPARTURE is fully protected under the copyright laws of the British Commonwealth, including Canada, the United States of America, and all other countries of the Copyright Union. All rights, including professional and amateur stage productions, recitation, lecturing, public reading, motion picture, radio broadcasting, television and the rights of translation into foreign languages are strictly reserved.

ISBN 978-0-573-12075-6

www.samuelfrench-london.co.uk

www.samuelfrench.com

For Amateur Production Enquiries

UNITED KINGDOM AND WORLD EXCLUDING NORTH AMERICA

plays@SamuelFrench-London.co.uk

020 7255 4302/01

Each title is subject to availability from Samuel French,

depending upon country of performance.

CAUTION: Professional and amateur producers are hereby warned that *DEPARTURE* is subject to a licensing fee. Publication of this play does not imply availability for performance. Both amateurs and professionals considering a production are strongly advised to apply to the appropriate agent before starting rehearsals, advertising, or booking a theatre. A licensing fee must be paid whether the title is presented for charity or gain and whether or not admission is charged.

The professional rights in this play are controlled by Samuel French Ltd, 52 Fitzroy Street, London W1T 5JR.

No one shall make any changes in this title for the purpose of production. No part of this book may be reproduced, stored in a retrieval system, or transmitted in any form, by any means, now known or yet to be invented, including mechanical, electronic, photocopying, recording, videotaping, or otherwise, without the prior written permission of the publisher. No one shall upload this title, or part of this title, to any social media websites.

The right of STEPHEN SMITH to be identified as author of this work has been asserted by him in accordance with Section 77 of the Copyright, Designs and Patents Act 1988.

DEPARTURE

First performed by Waterbeach Community Players at the Sawston Drama Festival on March 25th, 1988 with the following cast:

Rosemary Gibbs	Sue Blow
Mandy Gibbs	Catherine Jones
Dennis Tippitt	Chris Shinn
Sheila Tippitt	Rosemary Jolley

The play was directed by **Stephen Smith**
Designed by **Mark Easterfield**
With the assistance of Julie Petrucci, Tony Sawford, Judy Hanson, Stephen Cannie and Paula Cannie

CHARACTERS

Rosemary Gibbs
Mandy Gibbs
Dennis Tippitt
Sheila Tippitt

The action takes place in a corner of a departure lounge at Gatwick Airport

Time—the present

DEPARTURE

A Sunday afternoon in October in a secluded corner of a departure lounge at Gatwick Airport

Along the back and R are display boards advertising various airlines and duty-free goods. Two 3-seater benches are CS and a litter-bin is L. The whole area has been cordoned off to be cleaned and litter abounds. Various cleaning equipment has been left but the cleaners have gone for a break and there is a sign saying, "Cleaning in Progress". All entrances and exits are made L

As the CURTAIN *rises Rosemary Gibbs and her daughter Mandy, rush on ignoring the sign. Rosemary is in her forties. She has dyed black hair, large glasses and wears over-bright clothes. She has a large bandage on her leg and is carrying a shopping bag. Mandy is about twenty years younger than her mother and virtually a carbon copy*

Rosemary (*out of breath*) I think we'll be safe here, Mandy.
Mandy Yes, Mum.
Rosemary I don't know what came over that man.
Mandy No, Mum.

Mandy stands around gormlessly, while her mother surveys the untidy scene and then starts to tidy up and clean everything in sight

Rosemary Look! They don't keep these places clean enough. There's dust on the back of this seat. Some people just don't seem to have pride in their work anymore. What must foreigners think when they arrive here, seeing all this dust? They must think we are a bunch of mucky devils, that's what they must think.
Mandy Shall I help?
Rosemary No, it's all right Mandy. You're on holiday.
Mandy So are you.
Rosemary Mothers are never on holiday, Mandy. They may change their environment, but they are never on holiday. Hopefully, one day you'll find that out.

Mandy I don't know if I want to be a mother if it means I'll never get another holiday.
Rosemary That's not the attitude, Mandy. The joys of motherhood and marriage far outweigh the disadvantages. You want to make a mark on this world, don't you?
Mandy I suppose so.
Rosemary Then one of the best ways is to have children. When I'm dead and buried, my memory will live on through you. Besides you can't stay under my wing all your life—you must build your own nest before it's too late. We don't want you ending up on the shelf, do we?
Mandy No, Mum.
Rosemary Meeting people on holiday is the ideal time to get to know them—catch them off guard when they are away from their normal way of life. They don't have as many inhibitions and are desperate for friendships, for someone to talk to. That's your chance, Mandy.
Mandy Yes, Mum.
Rosemary You have been practising your smile, haven't you?
Mandy Yes, Mum. (*She forces a smile*)
Rosemary (*admiringly*) Ah!
Mandy All I can do is try my best.
Rosemary And that's all I can ask from you. Don't worry, you have one big advantage.
Mandy What's that?
Rosemary Me as your mother. Someone who makes friends easily, someone who people like to talk to. This is the environment in which I thrive. That's why we are here, away from everyone else, in case some poor soul is on their own in need of companionship.
Mandy I thought we came here because that rude man told you to sod off.

Rosemary hurriedly moves to clean the other seat

Rosemary Er ... no. You have to excuse him, Mandy. I think he was feeling unwell. He obviously didn't know what he was saying. After talking to him for half an hour, I noticed his face was turning a funny colour. I think he may have contracted some kind of erotic disease, so I thought it safest if we left him. We don't want to ruin our holiday, do we?

Departure

Mandy No, certainly not.
Rosemary There seems to be a lot of it about. I've noticed it in other people, too. It seems to affect people's temper. No doubt they'll find a cure for it in time. Now, how does that look? (*Surveying everything that she has just cleaned*)
Mandy Fit to eat your dinner off.
Rosemary Thank you Mandy and that's what we will do in a roundabout way. Come and take the weight off your feet.

They both sit down and Rosemary rummages around in her bag, eventually producing a packet of biscuits

    When you are on a journey ...
Mandy Always be prepared.
Rosemary That's right.
Mandy Like a Boy Scout.
Rosemary Girl Guides in our case, Mandy. Have a biscuit.
Mandy Thanks, Mum.
Rosemary Once started we will have to finish all these biscuits you know.
Mandy Why?
Rosemary Because you are not allowed to take food out of the country.
Mandy Why's that?
Rosemary Because of the risk of spreading rabies. If, for example, a Spaniard ate one of these biscuits, he could get rabies because his body isn't used to English food.
Mandy Does that mean we can get rabies from Spanish food?
Rosemary No, because we've had the injections.
Mandy Those tetanus injections?
Rosemary That's it. Tetanus is Spanish for rabies, Mandy. Now Spain has joined the EEC it should no longer be necessary because we'll all be eating the same food but it's best ...
Mandy To be on the safe side.
Rosemary Yes.
Mandy So that's why the doctor said we didn't need the injections.
Rosemary Yes, but as you heard me say, he's not the one that is going to go down with rabies if he's wrong.
Mandy He didn't like that, did he?
Rosemary No, he didn't. He said I was off my trolley; but I told

him I pay my VAT and I'm entitled to have as many tetanus injections as I like.

Mandy He had no answer to that, did he?

Rosemary No, we had him there, Mandy. I think I'll get up now—my bottom is still a bit sore. How's yours?

Mandy It's not too bad.

Rosemary It's worth it though, Mandy. At least tomorrow we can sit in a taverna and eat our sangria safe in the knowledge we won't get rabies.

Mandy Shall I go and spend these refreshment vouchers now?

Rosemary Why not? Waste not, want not.

Mandy (*laughingly*) A voucher in the hand is worth ten in the bush.

Rosemary (*pleased*) Well done, Mandy, very funny. Now, you go off and surprise me.

Mandy (*worried*) Aren't you coming?

Rosemary No, I'll go for a wander—see if there is anyone I can be a Good Samaritan to. I'll meet you back here in about ten minutes.

Mandy OK then, Mum.

She exits L

Rosemary notices a dirty mark on one of the seats and rubs vigorously until she is satisfied that it is clean

She packs up all her gear and exits

A few seconds later Dennis Tippitt enters. He is middle-aged and wears a dark suit. He is carrying a "British Airways" hold-all.

He is angrily murmuring to himself and keeps looking in the direction from which he has come. Eventually he sits down and takes out a copy of the News of the World. *He tuts as he reads it while continually looking offstage. Suddenly he sees someone coming and desperately tries to put away the newspaper but can't get the zip of the hold-all undone in time so he has to hide the newspaper under the seat*

Sheila, Dennis's wife, enters. She is a few years younger than him and more suitably dressed for a holiday in the sun. She is carrying a large handbag

Sheila (*without noticing the newspaper*) Ah, there you are, Dennis.

Departure

Dennis (*grumpily*) Yes.

Sheila sits down next to him

Sheila I thought I'd lost you.
Dennis No such luck.
Sheila You were supposed to keep an eye on my bag. You know bags are not allowed to be left unattended here.
Dennis I hardly think the ladies' toilets at Gatwick is a top terrorist target.
Sheila It wasn't outside the toilets—it was next to your seat.
Dennis Anyway, no self respecting terrorist would carry a bomb in a bag like that.
Sheila What's wrong with this bag? Mother gave it to me.
Dennis I stand corrected—it must have already been on active service.
Sheila Why did you move?
Dennis Nigerians.
Sheila What?
Dennis Bloody Nigerians, that's what.
Sheila Nigerians?
Dennis They must be breeding like rabbits. There are enough kids running amok in this departure lounge to keep open several village schools.
Sheila What are you on about?
Dennis Not that anybody cares anymore. We used to stick together in the old days but today it is all self. I don't want to get involved. I didn't see anything. It's nothing to do with me. Of course we are leaving ourselves wide open. That's what they want. It makes it easy, doesn't it?
Sheila What?
Dennis Divide and rule.
Sheila As per usual, Dennis, you are not making a word of sense.
Dennis That's what everyone says, but they'll find out when it's too late.
Sheila (*getting some knitting out of her bag*) Is it those children? Have they upset you?
Dennis I was perfectly happily reading my newspaper . . .
Sheila Something has upset you.
Dennis . . . and then one of them sits in your seat. Sneaks up on my blind side and sits in your seat.

Sheila Why didn't you say the seat was occupied?
Dennis Before I had realized what had happened they had me with a pincer movement. I was surrounded.
Sheila (*starting her knitting*) Are we talking about children or commandos?
Dennis They were waiting, you know.
Sheila (*as if talking to a child*) Were they?
Dennis Yes.
Sheila (*not taking a lot of notice*) What for?
Dennis For you to go to the loo.
Sheila I didn't go to the loo.
Dennis They weren't to know that.
Sheila Why were they waiting?
Dennis For you to vacate your seat.
Sheila (*stopping knitting*) Ah I see, it all makes sense now. This is the divide and rule part, yes? (*She starts knitting again*)
Dennis At last I'm getting through. We had prime seats: good view of the aircraft taking off; the television monitors with all the flight information changing every thirty seconds; and a long range view of the security checks in case anything exciting happened there.
Sheila I didn't realize that we were so privileged.

Dennis gets up and looks at the display boards

Dennis Airports are notorious places for long waits. I need things to keep a highly-tuned brain like mine active. Flights have been known to be delayed—not British ones of course, but unfortunately there are foreign airlines using this airport too.
Sheila (*in mock astonishment*) Really. Well, being with a British airline we have nothing to worry about then, do we?
Dennis But we're not, are we? How many times have I told you to buy British, to preserve our national heritage, and what do I find when I look at my ticket? We are flying with a Scandinavian airline.
Sheila Dan-Air!
Dennis I have nothing against them personally. They make fine butter and bacon, and that Bjorn Borg who plays the piano is quite funny; but flying is not one of their strong points. They are a seafaring nation. If we were going by boat, I may have

Departure 7

considered it, but flying in a Danish aircraft is taking an unnecessary risk.

Sheila Dennis, Dan-Air is British.

Dennis I think I know my airlines, Sheila, I was in the RAF during the war. If it was British it would have British in front of its name like British Airways. It's not British Dan-Air, is it?

Sheila No, Dennis.

Dennis If we had our original, well chosen seats, I could have pointed out all the different airlines to you.

Sheila That would have been interesting.

Dennis But it is not to be.

Sheila No.

Dennis Instead we have a prime view of the cleaning cupboard.

Sheila Such are the fortunes of war.

Dennis It's typical of your average Nigerian.

Sheila I hate to disappoint you, Dennis, but they weren't Nigerians.

Dennis They knew the only way they could get those seats was if one of us left for the call of nature.

Sheila (*getting irritated*) I did not go to the loo!

Dennis They have no respect for the citizens of the host nation. If it's a good position, they'll nab it. It is no coincidence that their embassy collects more parking tickets than any other. What is worse, they get away with it. Claim diplomatic immunity and so now they reckon they can park anywhere, whether they are in a car or not.

Sheila You've been reading those magazines again, haven't you?

Dennis They are clever, though. I have to take my hat off to them. First one nonchalantly wanders over to your seat. The youngest, go for the sympathy vote. I mean how can a fully grown adult like me scold a four-year-old Nigerian for innocently sitting in the wrong seat. (*Pause*) Of course he could have been a dwarf; but for all intents and purposes he looked like a four-year-old Nigerian.

Sheila Dennis, you have a wonderful way of making the simplest action seem like the opening page of a blockbusting epic. What is this one going to be called? *Gatwick Revisited*? Or *I Lost My Seat to a Junior Stormtrooper*?

Dennis (*taking no notice*) Then his brother joins him and I get

moved further along my seat; until eventually by sheer weight of numbers I'm forced to take refuge here.
Sheila It's a very touching story, Dennis, bound to be a best seller.
Dennis (*annoyed*) I might have just spoken to a brick wall for all the sympathy I get from you.
Sheila Sorry, Dennis.
Dennis No, you know what you're doing. I'll just keep quiet. Leave you to your knitting. Obviously that is all you need to stimulate your mind.
Sheila Oh no, Dennis, you keep talking—it does wonders to my pullovers. I work twice as fast when we're having a row. When I'm on my own, my mind wanders: I dream of having a cup of tea with Paul Newman, or visualize you skiing naked down the Matterhorn.
Dennis You don't even drink tea.
Sheila (*seductively*) That's what makes it all the more exciting.
Dennis (*deliberately changing the subject*) How do you know they are not Nigerians?
Sheila Because they are going to Entebbe.
Dennis We're going to Majorca, but that doesn't make us Spanish.
Sheila No, Dennis.
Dennis (*pause*) Where is Entebbe?
Sheila Uganda.
Dennis Well, they're all the same anyway, aren't they?
Sheila Who?
Dennis Africans. Unstable. Next week Entebbe could be in Nigeria.
Sheila If you moved it two thousand miles, yes, Dennis.
Dennis You know what I mean. They change their governments more often than I change my underpants.
Sheila Where did you get that newspaper?

Dennis hurriedly returns to his seat and puts his foot on the hidden paper

Dennis What newspaper?
Sheila The one you were supposedly happily reading prior to the Ugandan invasion.
Dennis Nigerian.

Departure

Sheila Whatever.
Dennis I bought it at the station while you went to the Ladies.
Sheila You've got an obsession with me going to the loo. I haven't been since we left home. I'm sure there must be a name for a person like you, a latrinist or something.
Dennis Where did you go then?
Sheila To see what platform our train was on.
Dennis Oh.
Sheila You must have hidden that newspaper. If you bought it at the station, how come I didn't see it?
Dennis I left it behind.
Sheila Convenient. Decoy was it? So that you could make your getaway before your Ugandan friends put you in the pot and served you as the inflight meal?
Dennis Don't be stupid.
Sheila What was it then?
Dennis How do you mean?
Sheila Watch my lips, Dennis. Which newspaper did you buy?
Dennis I can't remember offhand.
Sheila What do you mean, you can't remember? You're hiding something, aren't you? I know what it is: you sneaked off to buy the *News of the World*, didn't you?
Dennis Rubbish.
Sheila The great defender of moral values sneaked off to have a peek at the latest scandal, sexual outrages and topless women.
Dennis I did not buy the *News of the World*, Sheila. I wouldn't be seen dead with that filthy rag.
Sheila Huh!
Dennis What do you mean, "Huh"?
Sheila Last week, it was delivered to our house by mistake. The week before, Fred lent it to you because it had a good article on fishing.
Dennis It did!
Sheila You don't even go fishing, Dennis.
Dennis I'm interested. I don't have to do everything I'm interested in. I'm interested in boxing, but it doesn't mean I have to go twelve rounds with Frank Bruno.
Sheila You know you only get worked up reading it. If there's a banner headline about some woman in Penge having an affair with her alsatian, I get a week of lectures about how bad the

world is getting, and that all alsatians should now be neutered in case we breed a race of werewolves.

Dennis I don't know what on earth you're talking about.

Sheila They deliberately write stories like that for people like you.

Dennis People like me! What's that supposed to mean?

Sheila People who seem to be more outraged at what is supposedly happening in Penge than what is happening on their own doorstep.

Dennis Oh, so that's all the thanks I get for forking out over four hundred quid to give you a foreign holiday.

Sheila And you.

Dennis Did I ever say I wanted to go?

Sheila Not in so many words.

Dennis Not in any words. I'm doing this for you because you kept nagging me.

Sheila All I was trying to do was to give you a bit of advice that would get you out of this bigoted, narrow-minded phase you're going through.

Dennis gets up and walks away

Dennis I don't see the point in carrying on this conversation.

Sheila You always say that when you're losing. In fact, we always seem to be arguing these days and I think it's because we don't see enough of each other.

Dennis What nonsense!

Sheila No, hear me out. You are always away on business or down the golf club. We never really get a chance to relax with each other. Everything is so tense. You're waiting for me to jump down your throat and I'm waiting for you to make some inane comment.

Dennis (*sulkily*) I don't make inane comments.

Sheila It's not all me, Dennis. You've got to admit you're partly to blame. Why can't you think a bit more before you speak.

Dennis (*sarcastically*) Would you like me to tape my mouth up?

Sheila Don't be silly. You weren't always like this. You used to be witty and fun to be with. Now you're just a grumpy old sourpuss. To be honest, I can't stand it anymore. I have to keep making wisecracks to keep myself sane.

Dennis Oh, so I'm driving you insane now, am I?

Sheila gets up and goes towards him

Departure

Sheila The reason I so much wanted us to go on this holiday, is to find out if we can still live together for a week without coming to blows.

Dennis We could have done that in Blackpool.

Sheila In Blackpool, at the merest hint of trouble, one of us could have got the train home. In Majorca we will have to stick it out—through thick and thin, in sickness and in health.

Dennis You make it sound like marriage vows.

Sheila It is in a way. Let's face it, Dennis, our marriage is on the rocks.

Dennis No, it isn't.

Sheila What have we got then?

Dennis (*momentarily speechless*) Er ... er ... Oh, you women read too much of this Mills and Boon rubbish and expect marriage to be one long honeymoon. This is the real world, Sheila, not an episode of *Lady Chatterley's Lover*. (*He storms past her*)

Sheila I hope you're not implying I'm having an affair with the man who does our weeds. He must be at least ninety.

Dennis You know what I mean.

Sheila Oh, I know what you mean all right; but do you know what I mean? It may be OK for you spending all day at work but what about me? My highlight of the day is your triumphant return, whenever that might be, full of the joys of Spring or generally lack of them.

Dennis So it's OK for me at work is it? You haven't a clue the battle I have to go through every day, have you? Not only am I expected to sell a product that is being undercut by our rivals, but I am supposed to sell more each year. Every time I hit my sales target I am told, "Splendid Dennis, well done old chap. Now let's see if we can do even better next year". I am paid to be witty and charming all day with my customers, irrespective of what they say or do to me, but I don't see why I should continue acting when I'm in the privacy of my own home.

Sheila I appreciate you don't have an easy time at work, Dennis, but if you're going to take it out on me then perhaps we should be adult and call it a day.

Dennis (*shocked*) Get a divorce?

Sheila Yes.

Rosemary enters

Rosemary Excuse me, are these seats taken?

Dennis flings himself onto the seat

Dennis Yes.
Sheila (*at the same time*) No.
Rosemary Pardon?
Sheila (*sternly*) Dennis.
Dennis (*to Rosemary*) No.
Rosemary Oh, good. It's chaos over there, all those little children running about.
Dennis Told you. That's three nil to them.
Rosemary Pardon?
Sheila My husband seems to have got the idea into his head that those African children are trying to take over the departure lounge.
Rosemary Why?
Sheila Good question.
Rosemary If you ask me, they are just high-spirited kids going home.
Dennis Nobody asked you.
Sheila Don't take any notice of Dennis, he hates simple explanations. By the way, my name is Sheila.

They shake hands

Rosemary Rosemary. Rosemary Gibbs.

Sheila goes behind the seat

Sheila As you have gathered, this is my husband, Dennis.
Rosemary (*offering her hand*) How do you do.

Dennis doesn't respond

Sheila Dennis!

Dennis reluctantly gets up to shake hands

Dennis Pleased to meet you I'm sure.
Rosemary (*seeing the newspaper under Dennis's seat*) Do you know you've dropped your newspaper?
Dennis (*unconvincingly*) Oh, what's that doing there?
Sheila What is it, Dennis?

Dennis picks up the newspaper and quickly sits on it

Departure

Dennis Some discarded newspaper.
Rosemary Wasn't it the *News of the World*?
Dennis Possibly. Somone's obviously left it behind.

Rosemary laughs and sits next to him

Rosemary And now it's on your left behind.
Dennis (*not amused*) Yes.
Rosemary That's strange, because I was here only a few minutes ago and it wasn't there then.
Sheila (*from behind him*) That is strange. Isn't it Dennis?
Dennis (*embarrassed*) Yes.
Sheila (*glorying in Dennis's embarrassment and running her fingers through his hair*) How do you account for that?
Dennis (*sharply*) How am I supposed to know?

Sheila moves away from him

Sheila You haven't joined the Masons, have you?
Dennis (*annoyed as he knows Sheila is enjoying herself*) No.
Sheila I just wondered if it was one of their special forms of greeting: sitting on a copy of the *News of the World* until a fellow Mason wiggled his little finger at you. (*She wiggles her finger*)

Dennis gets up annoyed and then sits down very quickly when he realizes the newspaper is showing

Dennis You think this is very funny, don't you?
Sheila Surely you see the funny side, Dennis? Particularly as you wouldn't be seen dead with the *News of the World* but seem quite content to remain sitting on it while alive.

Dennis throws the newspaper to the floor and Sheila gingerly picks it up and takes it over to the bin L

Rosemary (*to Dennis*) I have my daughter, Mandy, with me but our flight has been delayed for two hours, so she has gone to spend our refreshment vouchers. Operational reasons they called it, whatever that means.
Dennis It means they are not operational, that's what it means. These days all these fancy titles mean the reverse of what they say, like Industrial Action which really means industrial inaction.
Rosemary Or Fun Run?

Dennis What?
Rosemary Well I can't see what fun there is in running. I used to hate cross-country at school. Not that girls had to do cross-country at our school. It was just that I fancied this really good looking long-distance runner.
Dennis That wasn't quite what I meant.

Sheila joins them on the seat

Sheila So your only chance of meeting him was on cross-country runs?
Rosemary I wouldn't exactly call it meeting him—seeing him disappearing into the distance would be more accurate. He was always changed and off home before I could ever complete the course. He had a lovely bum though! For first three hundred yards I was in ecstasy—after that I got a stitch.
Dennis (*changing the subject*) Being delayed, I assume you're travelling with one of these incompetent foreign airlines that tend to clutter up the sky.
Rosemary Dan-Air.
Dennis I thought so, they should have stuck to longboats.
Rosemary I didn't know they were foreign.
Dennis It's an easy mistake to make; my wife made it too.
Sheila Where are you going?
Rosemary Nowhere at the moment.
Sheila On holiday, I mean.
Rosemary Oh sorry, Palma.
Sheila So are we.
Rosemary (*pleased*) Well you'll be on the same flight then.
Sheila We didn't hear any announcements.
Rosemary No, they don't make them for flights anymore—it's all flashed up on those television screens over there. (*She points* L)
Dennis (*sarcastically*) Seasoned traveller, know all about it, do you?
Sheila (*reprimanding*) Dennis.
Rosemary No, it's just that they've got signs up everywhere saying so.
Dennis Oh.
Rosemary What flight number are you?
Sheila Dennis?
Dennis How do I know.

Departure 15

Sheila Look at the ticket. For such an expert on airports, you do seem to lack the fundamentals.
Dennis All right, I'm looking. *He takes from his pocket a wallet with all the holiday documents in but can't see the flight number on the ticket until Rosemary points it out to him, much to his disgust)* DA Four Seven Eight. *He flings the wallet into Sheila's lap while she starts knitting again)*
Rosemary Snap.

Dennis angrily gets up and goes towards the entrance

Dennis You see the effects those flaming Nigerians are having on our holiday? They are out to cause civil unrest. We could have missed our plane.
Sheila I can't see how we could have missed our plane if it's been delayed.
Dennis That is not the point. They have deprived us of information.
Rosemary If you go to Gatwick Handling desk with your boarding card, they'll give you a one pound fifty refreshment voucher.
Sheila Off you go then, Dennis.
Dennis Why me?
Sheila Give you a chance for a progress report on your Nigerians. They could have advanced on the Duty Free Shop by now.
Dennis Perhaps I could do with stretching my legs. I'll check the information on those TV screens.

He goes back to the seat to pick up his holdall and starts to exit

Sheila *(happily knitting)* Don't forget the tickets, love.

Rosemary picks them up from Sheila's lap and hands them to Dennis as he returns grudgingly

Dennis *(out of the corner of his mouth)* We're not on holiday yet, you know.
Sheila I was just practising.

Dennis exits

Rosemary Friends of yours, are they?
Sheila Who?
Rosemary The Nigerians.

Sheila Ugandans, actually. No. Dennis has an obsession about them.
Rosemary Oh, I am sorry.
Sheila He thinks they are about to mount a coup in the departure lounge.
Rosemary Yes, these people do have strange habits. It's all to do with their religion. We have to learn to be compassionate about these sorts of things: live and let live. It's just a pity they tend to do it in public—would be much better in the privacy of their own homes.
Sheila (*stopping knitting*) No, I don't quite think . . .
Rosemary Personally, I think it's a bit cruel to the chicken, but we mustn't interfere in other people's cultures.
Sheila (*somewhat mystified*) No.
Rosemary Is your husband afraid of flying?
Sheila (*starting knitting again*) I shouldn't think so.
Rosemary It's just I'm not usually wrong about people and I would say that he was uptight about something. As we are in an airport, it usually means flying.
Sheila He hasn't said anything to me.
Rosemary He wouldn't; he's a proud man, isn't he?
Sheila Stubborn is a better description.
Rosemary Have you any children?
Sheila No.
Rosemary So you haven't a son in his late twenties or early thirties?
Sheila No, why?
Rosemary No reason. I have a daughter, Mandy.
Sheila So you said.
Rosemary I'd show you a photo of her but it doesn't do her any justice. She's had the braces taken off now and I somehow managed to spill some jam on it.
Sheila Oh dear.
Rosemary Anyway you'll be able to see her in the flesh soon.
Sheila (*forced*) Oh, good.
Rosemary My pride and joy she is. (*Pause*) Trouble with you, was it?
Sheila Trouble?
Rosemary With your tubes or anything.
Sheila (*shocked*) Pardon?

Departure

Rosemary Why you haven't had any children.
Sheila (*embarrassed*) No.
Rosemary Husband didn't want any?
Sheila You could say that.
Rosemary They can be selfish sods at times, depriving a woman of her natural function.
Sheila I wouldn't say ...
Rosemary Of course you can cheat on them—pretend to forget to take the pill and all that, but they always find out in the end.
Sheila Do they?
Rosemary In the middle of a row, you let it slip. For a moment you feel superior, you know, because you have complete control over that sort of thing, but they never forget and from then on every time the child does anything wrong you get the blame.
Sheila Really.
Rosemary Not that I know that much about sex. I didn't know what a lesbian was until I was thirty-five. Came as quite a shock, I can tell you—particularly as I was in Sainsbury's at the time.
Sheila (*edging away*) Yes, it would.
Rosemary You see my husband died many years ago. When Mandy was ten.
Sheila I am sorry.
Rosemary I'm over it now, of course; but you do feel as though you've missed something from life, don't you?
Sheila I suppose you do.
Rosemary Not that it's happened to you.
Sheila I wouldn't exactly say that.
Rosemary Oh look, here comes Mandy.

Mandy enters

Mandy There you are Mum. (*She hands Rosemary a roll*)
Rosemary Thank you, Mandy. What is it?

Mandy sits next to her mother, where Dennis had been formerly

Mandy It's called a turkey cannon.
Rosemary (*looking at it*) What's it got in it?
Mandy Turkey.
Rosemary Oh, well, might as well give it a whirl. (*She takes a large bite*)

Mandy They were one ninety-five each so you owe me ninety pence.
Rosemary Right. Now Mandy, this is Sheila.
Mandy How do you do. (*She shakes Sheila's hand*)
Sheila Very well, thank you. (*She looks down at her hand when she realizes that Mandy's hands are greasy*)
Mandy You know those noisy little kids.
Rosemary Yes, Mandy. Funnily enough, we were just talking about them. Weren't we, Sheila?
Sheila Yes.
Mandy Well you should see what they're doing with this middle aged man.
Sheila Oh, dear. Is he sort of grumpy-looking, with a dark suit on?
Mandy Yes, that's the one. He seems to be playing a game with them.

Sheila gets up and moves across stage to L, *looking for Dennis*

Rosemary How do you mean?
Mandy What's that game called with a pole in the middle and lots of pieces of ribbon coming off it, which everyone grabs and dances around?
Rosemary No idea, Mandy. Everything has changed since the schools went comprehensive.
Mandy Well this man seems to be the pole.
Sheila Oh dear.
Mandy You know him?
Sheila Vaguely.
Rosemary It's her husband.
Mandy (*getting up*) Shall I show you where he is?
Sheila (*returning to her seat*) Er ... no, better leave him.
Rosemary I think it wise—could be nasty when they get the chicken out.
Mandy (*sitting down*) Will it be hot in Spain, Mum?
Rosemary Hope so, Mandy, but it is the end of the season so we can't expect miracles. (*To Sheila*) Being a one-parent family I can't afford to go in high season.
Sheila No, quite.
Rosemary Late booking with you, was it?
Sheila Sort of.
Rosemary Suddenly fancied a week in the sun?

Departure

Sheila Yes.
Rosemary Once he's untangled himself, I wonder what your husband will get you with the voucher.
Sheila I've no idea.
Rosemary He looks like a tuna fish man to me.
Sheila Does he?
Rosemary Yes, and I'm not usually wrong about people, am I, Mandy?
Mandy No, Mum.
Rosemary I bet he'll come back with tuna fish rolls, you mark my words.
Sheila We'll see.
Rosemary Assuming they do tuna fish rolls. Do they do tuna fish rolls, Mandy?
Mandy I don't know.
Rosemary Didn't you look?
Mandy No, I got one of these because everyone else was getting one. I thought they must be good if they're popular.
Rosemary Being popular doesn't necessarily make something good, Mandy. Curries are popular, but eat too many of them and your kidneys rot away.
Mandy Ugh, I won't eat any more of them, then.
Rosemary Once in a while is OK. Everything in moderation, Mandy. But this modern living, away from traditional English food, will in the end ruin your organs. Remember, in your grandad's day there were no such things as Chinese take-aways or curry houses; kidney transplants were unheard of.
Mandy I'll remember that, Mum.
Rosemary Good.

She hands her half-eaten roll to Mandy and gets up to shake the crumbs off her dress and into the bin L

You know that is typical of my Mandy. It is her down to a tee.
Sheila What is?
Rosemary No imagination, just follow the common herd. That's why we both work at the Co-op, I expect. She works there because I do and I can't leave because she works there.
Sheila Catch 22.
Rosemary No, the Co-op. However hard I try, and I've tried hard, I think she lacks a father's influence. I don't care what people

say, all those feminists and everything, but I think there is no substitute for a father. I have tried to do my best, taken Mandy to football matches, fishing, down the pub, all the things her father would have done, but it's not the same. She lacks the aggression, that will to get to the front of the queue or fight for the last bargain in a sale.

Mandy (*embarrassed*) Mum!

Rosemary Eat your roll, Mandy or you'll get dyslexic. No, I think she is still too feminine, too nice. She needs to be much harder if she is going to survive in today's world. At the moment the only way she'll survive is to stay with me or find a husband and we all know she can't stay with me for ever, so I've got to find her a husband. That's why it's a pity you haven't got an eligible son.

Sheila (*just about had enough*) I think I better find out if Dennis needs rescuing.

Rosemary (*sitting down*) No need, he's coming this way.

Sheila (*disappointed*) Oh, yes.

Dennis enters

Dennis If I had my way I'd hang all those kids, the whole lot of them. They shouldn't be allowed in an airport terminal. They're under-age for a start. They just run wild like a bunch of animals, but what can you expect when they've got African parents.

Rosemary Oh dear, is your husband prejudiced?

Sheila I wouldn't exactly say that. Whatever colour, creed or culture, Dennis doesn't discriminate, he hates the lot.

Dennis I don't think that is very funny, Sheila. For the second time this afternoon I have been humiliated by those children and all you can do is make fun of it.

Sheila gets up and goes over to him

Sheila Well, it's all over now dear, and we can eat our rolls in peace. Assuming you did get two rolls.

Dennis Would you believe the cheapest one was one pound ninety-five. It's like those duty frees, a big con. They give you a voucher for one pound fifty and you have to pay another forty-five pence before you can buy anything. I'm certainly not paying one pound ninety-five for a morsel of turkey, a mouldy roll and a lettuce leaf.

Rosemary and Mandy look at the remainders of their rolls

Departure

It probably only cost forty-five pence in the first place.
Sheila (*angrily*) Well it's only going to cost you forty-five pence, isn't it.
Dennis That's not the point. I object to being taken for a ride at an airport. Particularly as I didn't want the roll in the first place.
Sheila What about me?
Dennis You can have something on the plane.
Sheila Because it's free. God, you can be really stingy, Dennis.
Dennis Careful is the word, Sheila. If you had your way there would be nothing left for our retirement. Anyway, I can't see why you're getting so worked up over a roll.
Sheila If we're going to sit here for another two hours, I'm getting something to eat. Where are those vouchers?
Dennis You'll need money.
Sheila Not if you don't want anything because that means I've got three pounds to spend (*she grabs the vouchers*) and I'm going to spend them.

Sheila exits. Dennis starts to chase after her and then gives up and returns to the seat to be faced by Rosemary

Rosemary (*after a pause*) No tuna fish.
Dennis (*bemused*) What?
Rosemary Nothing.

Dennis sits down in the middle of the other seat then gets up to take a book out of his hold-all which is under Rosemary's seat L

Rosemary We're at the Hotel Sanchez in Magaluff. It's only a two-star but being a one-parent family it was the best I could afford.
Dennis (*starting to read the book*) How nice for you.
Rosemary I'm sure we'll like it. We're easily pleased, aren't we, Mandy?
Mandy Yes, Mum.
Rosemary This is my daughter, Mandy, by the way.

Mandy gets up and waves

Dennis I noticed.

Rosemary moves to Dennis's seat

Rosemary You're not very happy are you?

Dennis How observant. (*He moves as far from Rosemary as possible*)
Rosemary The flying is it?
Dennis Certainly not.
Rosemary It's nothing to be ashamed of—many famous people are. Mandy's Uncle Ted was. That's my deceased husband's brother. Not that he was famous. (*Pause*) He was a conker champion at school once though.
Dennis (*gritting his teeth*) I am not afraid of flying.
Rosemary It really is a state of mind.

Mandy gets up to move across too

Mandy It's the safest way to fly.
Rosemary It's the only way to fly. Mandy, read your phrase-book.

Mandy reluctantly returns to her seat and takes a phrase-book from her handbag

It's just that when a plane crashes and say five hundred people get killed it makes the headlines because that's a lot all in one go. However, over the year thousands are killed on the roads but generally only in twos and threes so nobody notices. When my husband was killed it only made page seven of the *Dagenham Evening Telegraph*, below a story about a man exposing himself and above a review of the local gang show.
Dennis That's very reassuring.
Rosemary I thought it would be. Your only practical problem with flying is your ears.
Dennis My ears.
Rosemary Not just yours, but anyone's. They tend to pop at altitude. Now don't ask me why, because I don't know, but the best thing is a boiled sweet.
Dennis In my ears?
Rosemary No, not in your ears, you silly man. In your mouth, you suck it. You'd look a right wally with boiled sweets sticking out of your ears. Wouldn't he, Mandy?
Mandy Yes, Mum.

They both laugh

Rosemary Would you like Mandy to get you some?

Mandy gets up again expectantly

Departure

Dennis No, thank you.
Rosemary To be on the safe side.
Dennis No.
Rosemary It's no trouble, is it Mandy?
Mandy No, Mum.
Dennis (*angrily to Mandy*) Look, I am perfectly happy reading my book, thank you.

Mandy sits down again

Rosemary Sorry to contradict you, Dennis, but you don't look happy. Is it because you haven't got any children?
Dennis No, it is not.
Rosemary You don't look fulfilled to me. I don't think Sheila is fulfilled either.
Dennis Look, I do not want any children, I do not need any children and I have no desire for any children. Satisfied?
Rosemary Yes.
Dennis There are too many children in the world already without me adding to them.
Rosemary You have a point there, Dennis. Me and my husband, we only had the one because we didn't want to be a burden on the state. He was out of work at the time you see. Actually on our only trip abroad, as a family, when Jack got his job at Ford's, we nearly lost Mandy. We were in Rimini, in Italy, and she was run over by a German in a pedalo. He was very apologetic, well it sounded apologetic, we couldn't understand a word he was saying but Mandy had to be treated for concussion. I sometimes think that is why she only got one 'O' level. Anyway, at the time Jack and I thought should we have another one, to be on the safe side you know, but it never came to pass because he got put back on the night-shift.
Dennis (*to himself*) Thank God.
Rosemary Yes, thank God Mandy recovered and is the healthy girl you see before you. Have you ever been to Italy?
Dennis No.
Rosemary Nice country.
Dennis Is it?
Rosemary Well, it was when we were there. You ought to go sometime.
Dennis I have no desire to go to Italy thank you.

Rosemary I'm sure Spain will be just as nice.
Dennis Good.
Rosemary Why did you choose Spain?
Dennis I didn't.
Rosemary Sheila did, did she?
Dennis Yes.
Rosemary And you wanted to go somewhere else.
Dennis No, I didn't want to go anywhere.
Rosemary Oh, I see. That is why you are in a mood.

Dennis stands and tries to put his book back in his hold-all but the zip has jammed again

Dennis I am not in a mood. Could you kindly stop poking your nose in where it is not wanted. Why can't you go and harass someone else? This airport is full of people; surely I've had my share.
Rosemary Don't get upset, Dennis, I'm not harassing you, I'm just being friendly. You must have a persecution complex.
Dennis (*storming around in a boiling rage*) I do not have a persecution complex. I defy anyone to sit with you for ten minutes without going insane. All I have had is continual questions, anecdotes and general drivel. I couldn't give a monkey's whether Mandy's great uncle Albert was a conker champion or a world freestyle crocodile-juggling drag artist.

Mandy finally goes to join her mother

Mandy He's beginning to sound just like that other bloke.
Rosemary Yes I think Mandy is right, Dennis. Perhaps you should go and see the airport doctor, there seems to be a strange disease about.
Dennis Yes I know; it's you.

Rosemary gets up and goes over to him

Rosemary No, sorry Dennis, there is nothing wrong with me. It's the fear of flying that is getting you worked up. Perhaps the airport doctor can give you a tranquillizer.
Dennis I don't believe this. You have not listened to a word I have said, have you?
Rosemary Of course I have, Dennis; how could I hold a conversa-

tion with you without listening? I think we have been getting on very well and together we'll crack this fear don't worry.
Dennis Do you know you are a lunatic? You should be locked up.

Rosemary leads him to his seat and sits him down

Rosemary Now you have nothing to fear, Dennis. I'll be sitting next to you on the plane, I'll even hold your hand if you want.
Dennis (*in a near state of panic*) You are sitting next to me on the plane!
Rosemary Yes, isn't that lucky.

Dennis lets out a squeal of fright and bites hard on the hold-all he is clutching

Rosemary I glanced at your boarding card and you're sitting next to me. I assume Sheila has the window seat, so you'll be a thorn between two roses, isn't that cosy!
Dennis (*in a state of shock*) Perhaps I should go and see the airport doctor.
Rosemary I think it is best. (*She points Dennis in the right direction*) Now I happened to notice where it was when I came in. It's down there, the blue door on the left.

Dennis exits

Mandy (*looking at her phrase-book*) Mum, what's a "siesta"?
Rosemary I think dad used to make them at Ford's.
Mandy So it's a car then.
Rosemary (*starting to tidy up again*) Yes.
Mandy But it says you can only have them between twelve and four.
Rosemary No, that's a misprint. What is should say is that you can't have them between twelve and four on account of the heat. You see it's the hottest time of day and melts the tyres.
Mandy Oh, I see. Pretty bad getting that wrong. We could read this book, go out in our Ford Siesta and be involved in an accident because of a misprint.
Rosemary Printing trade is not what it used to be. That was probably printed in Hong Kong.
Mandy Do they speak Spanish in Hong Kong?
Rosemary No, that's why they make mistakes like that.

Sheila enters with a roll

Sheila Where's Dennis?
Rosemary Gone to see the airport doctor.
Sheila (*surprised*) Why?
Rosemary His fear of flying got the better of him.
Sheila His what?
Rosemary He just went to pieces, started rambling on about crocodile-juggling drag artists, almost went into a second childhood. I've never seen a man just crumble in front of my eyes as he did. Have you, Mandy?
Mandy No, not as quick as that.
Rosemary As you know, Sheila, I'm not usually wrong about people and if you want my opinion, I'd say that he was on the verge of a nervous breakdown.
Sheila Are you sure?
Rosemary The fear of flying is probably only the tip of the iceberg; I think it is more than that. We didn't have a chance to chat for too long but he is plainly upset about not having any children.
Sheila What?
Rosemary Oh yes, he went on at length about that. If it's not too late I would try for one, Sheila. Don't tell him though it would make a nice surprise.
Sheila (*not believing her ears*) This is Dennis you are talking about?
Rosemary Yes.
Sheila My husband, Dennis?
Rosemary Yes. I can understand it may be difficult for you to comprehend. Dennis has obviously been your rock of Gibraltar; you have looked up to him for support, strength and guidance.
Sheila I have?
Rosemary In your heart of hearts you know you have. But all great supports can crack in a storm and let's face it, your Dennis is a highly-strung man.
Sheila (*starting to take Rosemary seriously*) He does get uptight and starts worrying over trivial things.
Rosemary I noticed that.
Sheila Things that really he shouldn't be worrying about. These Ugandan children, for example. Who in their right mind would go on about them and get as worked up as Dennis has?

Departure

Rosemary Who indeed. It is a classic sign of someone heading for a nervous breakdown, isn't it, Mandy?
Mandy Classic, yes.
Rosemary It just needs one thing, Sheila, and they snap like a twig, collapse like a pack of cards ...
Mandy Erupt like an earthquake.
Rosemary Volcano, Mandy, erupt like a volcano. Earthquakes don't erupt.
Mandy Sorry, Mum. I always get that one wrong.
Sheila I threatened to leave him, you know. I bet that's what brought all this on.
Rosemary It all adds up Sheila.
Sheila That must be it. He must finally have listened to what I said.
Rosemary With devastating results.
Sheila Perhaps I was too harsh with him.
Rosemary Funny isn't it how people always seem to die leaving loved ones behind regretting their last words. I told my father he couldn't race pigeons to save his life and the next day a freak wind blew a swan through our front window, straight into my father's chair.
Sheila Killing him?
Rosemary No he was out buying *Pigeon Fancier Weekly*. But if he had heeded my words he could have been dead.
Sheila I think I'd better go and find Dennis.
Rosemary Good idea, comfort him in his hour of need.
Sheila He may not show it but he does need me, doesn't he?
Rosemary More than anyone else, and of course I could be wrong about the nervous breakdown.
Sheila Let's hope so.
Rosemary It could be something pushing against his brain, that's inclined to make people irritable.
Sheila Oh, my God.

Sheila hurriedly exits

Rosemary (*sitting down and rummaging through her bag*) Makes you feel good inside doesn't it, Mandy, to help people.
Mandy Yes, Mum.
Rosemary Sometimes I think that must be what I was put on this earth to do.

Mandy Yes, you certainly have an effect on a lot of people's lives.
Rosemary Thank you, Mandy, I try my best. (*She looks at her watch*) Now, we've still got over an hour, let's see if there is someone else we can help.

They both get up and wander off L

the CURTAIN *falls*

FURNITURE AND PROPERTY LIST

On stage: Display boards advertising airlines and duty-free goods
Two 3-seater benches
Bin
Sign saying "Cleaning in Progress"
Cleaning equipment: bucket, mop, dusters, etc.
Rope

Off stage: Two rolls **(Mandy)**
One roll **(Sheila)**

Personal: **Rosemary:** watch; shopping bag. *In it:* biscuits
Mandy: handbag. *In it:* phrase-book
Dennis: wallet containing plane ticket; British Airways zip-fastened hold-all. *In it:* newspaper (the *News of the World*), book
Sheila: handbag. *In it:* knitting

LIGHTING PLOT

One interior setting. No practical fittings required

To open: Interior lighting

No cues

MADE AND PRINTED IN GREAT BRITAIN BY
LATIMER TREND & COMPANY LTD PLYMOUTH
MADE IN ENGLAND

www.ingramcontent.com/pod-product-compliance
Lightning Source LLC
Chambersburg PA
CBHW070454050426
42450CB00012B/3278